THE MAGIC PLACE

A SIMPLE GUIDE TO BEING HAPPY, EVEN IF LIFE GETS A LITTLE CRAPPY

ELISE MORGAN

THE MAGIC PLACE

A SIMPLE GUIDE TO BEING HAPPY, EVEN IF LIFE GETS A LITTLE CRAPPY

© 2025 ALL RIGHTS RESERVED.

Published by She Rises Studios Publishing **www.SheRisesStudios.com**.

No part of this book may be reproduced or transmitted in any form whatsoever, electronic, or mechanical, including photocopying, recording, or by any informational storage or retrieval system without the expressed written, dated, and signed permission from the publisher and author.

LIMITS OF LIABILITY/DISCLAIMER OF WARRANTY:

The author and publisher of this book have used their best efforts in preparing this material. While every attempt has been made to verify the information provided in this book, neither the author nor the publisher assumes any responsibility for any errors, omissions, or inaccuracies.

The author and publisher make no representation or warranties with respect to the accuracy, applicability, or completeness of the contents of this book. They disclaim any warranties (expressed or implied), merchantability, or for any purpose. The author and publisher shall in no event be held liable for any loss or other damages, including but not limited to special, incidental, consequential, or other damages.

ISBN: 978-1-968061-43-2

DEDICATION

*I would like to dedicate this book to my late sister,
Patti Lyn Wilensky, who died by suicide at the young age of 18.
If I can help even just ONE person empower themselves enough to
change their mindset, so that they can
LIVE A HAPPY AND PURPOSEFUL LIFE,
then my sister's death will NOT be in vain.*

Patti, I love you and will always miss you…

Till we meet again on the other side.

ACKNOWLEDGMENTS

First and foremost, I would like to thank my biggest fan. My amazing, fully supporting, loving, and truly understanding husband, Michael Morgan.

He supports me through all my "animated" daily antics, all my temperature change moments (I'm usually freezing), my sometimes tears, my wise-ass joking around, my excitement, and TALKING about my business and any other subject because I do talk A LOT...

He truly is my King, and I cherish our life together.

I would also like to thank my handsome sons, Austin and West. You both are my big supporters behind the scenes, and know that I am truly trying to help the world! Both of you are truly my greatest gifts in life. I am so grateful to be your mom.

I also want to thank my friends, family, and coaching mentors who support my current coaching/speaking/book writing/podcasting endeavors! It means the world to me that you understand and support what I am trying to accomplish!

I am also truly grateful to anyone who buys and reads this book because that means you have made the decision to take control of your life, be HAPPY, live the life of your DREAMS, and to take action to do it.

YOU ARE WORTHY AND DESERVING!

TABLE OF CONTENTS

Introduction 11

Preface 13

Chapter One: The Law Of Attraction 17

Chapter Two: Your Thoughts Create Your Reality 19

Chapter Three: Visualization 21

Chapter Four: Awareness 23

Chapter Five: The Power Of I Am… 25

Chapter Six: Stop Giving Your Power Away 27

Chapter Seven: Accountability 29

Chapter Eight: Alignment 33

Chapter Nine: Who Are You? The True Authentic You 35

Chapter Ten: Action 37

Chapter Eleven: Gratitude 39

Conclusion 43

Bonus Journal 45

INTRODUCTION

Hello! I'm Elise Morgan, a Professional Figure Athlete/Personal Trainer and Fitness Model turned Certified Life Coach, NLP Practitioner, Podcaster, Author, and Transformational Speaker.

I am here to help you LOVE YOUR LIFE!! NO MATTER WHAT!!

I learned to do what I do:

After people-pleasing, after putting myself last, after not loving or respecting myself, after divorce, after toxic relationships, after abuse, after betrayal, after the death of loved ones, after my sister's suicide, after multiple miscarriages, after a broken back, after a DUI, after bankruptcy… AFTER ALL THE THINGS I WENT THROUGH.

After going through these things and more, I developed and learned some steps to keep me feeling happy and grateful no matter what is going on around me… It's like a MAGIC PLACE… and I wrote this guide to share them with YOU… so that YOU can start to feel happy TODAY, no matter what challenge you are facing or what you may be feeling about yourself, or if you rely on others for your happiness.

RELYING on another human to make and keep you happy is, well, limiting and sometimes very disappointing… hence feeling sad a lot of the time!

Which is why I've learned how to make MYSELF happy... PERIOD.!!!!!

Sounds SO crazy, I know!!!! The truth is, if we can figure out the mind stuff that's going on WITHIN, then we can feel happy, confident, and purposeful, instead of feeling sad, alone, and defeated... Pretty cool, right?

I know this journey has been LIFE-CHANGING for me and now for so many of my clients, and it's why I wrote this guide.

The fact that you bought this guide indicates to me that you don't want to feel so sad, disappointed, defeated, ALL THE FEELINGS you are feeling all the time ANYMORE...

So... Let's get to it...

NO TURNING BACK AFTER THIS!

YOU ARE ABOUT TO LEARN ABOUT THE MAGIC PLACE!

PREFACE

Here are some of the things I hear from Young Adults, Men, and Women.

These examples are just a SMIDGE of all the struggles that you may be going through, and each can and does interchange between the ages and sexes.

YOUNG ADULTS:

"I hate my life! I feel so much pressure from my parents and teachers that I always feel so stressed and anxious!"

"I'm worried about my grades."

"My boyfriend/girlfriend broke up with me… I feel so heartbroken… I'm nothing without them!"

"It's so hard to find a job, they want experience, but I'm fresh out of college… I'm worried about paying off my student loans and rent without a job."

"I always feel sad, I don't want to get out of bed or do anything."

"I'm worried about my future."

"That girl/guy is better than me, smarter than me, better looking."

"I don't like myself."

"I always feel so anxious."

MEN:

"I'm afraid to show my emotions, I think I will appear weak."

"I feel so much pressure to provide for my family… The kids are driving me crazy, and my wife is always nagging."

"I feel like it's the end of my life since my wife left me."

"I'm just not happy in this rat race. I thought I wanted to be (insert occupation here), but I'm miserable and stuck here."

"I am bored."

WOMEN:

"I feel like a doormat. Everyone else comes before me and treats me as such."

"I am in an abusive relationship, but I'm stuck here with no way out."

"My marriage just ended, and now I am a single mom, and I'm scared to death."

"My kids are grown and moved out, and now I don't even know who I am or what to do with my life."

"I hate the way I look and feel."

"I feel like I'm middle-aged and too old to start over."

I can go on and on with what YOU may be feeling and struggling with. This guide is your answer to feeling better and knowing what steps to take to get through what you are going through and BEYOND, because this guide teaches how to live your life HAPPY, no matter what challenges you face or what dreams you want to chase.

Even if you're not currently facing any challenges or struggles in life, incorporating the steps from this book into your daily routine will foster lasting mental well-being and inner peace. These practices will help you maintain a healthy, balanced life, equipping you with the skills to preserve this sense of well-being, no matter what's happening around you.

CHAPTER ONE

THE LAW OF ATTRACTION

The Law of Attraction states that whatever you focus on, think about, read about, and talk about intensely, you're going to attract more into your life.

– Jack Canfield

This guide and my coaching are based on the Law of Attraction. I KNOW it sounds a little "WOO WOO" but try to have an open mind.

So, what is the LAW OF ATTRACTION?

The law of attraction is a popular concept in self-improvement and spirituality that states that people can attract positive experiences and outcomes into their lives through their thoughts and emotions. The basic idea is that our thoughts and feelings create a vibration that attracts similar experiences and outcomes into our lives.

According to the law of attraction, if you focus on positive thoughts and feelings, you will attract positive experiences and outcomes into your life, and if you focus on negative thoughts and feelings, you will attract negative experiences and outcomes.

Some proponents of the law of attraction suggest that it can be used to attract abundance, happiness, and success, while others claim that it can be used to manifest specific desires, such as a dream job, a new car, or a loving relationship.

We are all vibrational energy beings, and our thoughts are vibrational, so what the law of attraction actually is saying and what seems to be scientifically proven is:

LIKE ATTRACTS LIKE

So, if you are always in a negative vibration (feeling) and are stuck there, don't know how to get out, that is where the momentum of your thoughts is, hence keeping you stuck and unhappy!

Your thoughts about basically anything are truly POWERFUL and become YOUR TRUTH.

Where your thought energy goes… basically GROWS.

So, the more you think negatively, the more those thoughts and vibrations grow, hence bringing more and more negative to you. On the contrary, positive thinking is a high frequency, and the more you're in that vibration, the more good comes to you…

It's like magic!

CHAPTER TWO

YOUR THOUGHTS CREATE YOUR REALITY

Change your thoughts and you change your world.

– Norman Vincent Peale

The idea that our thoughts create our reality is a powerful one, as it suggests that we have the ability to shape and control our own experiences through the power of our thoughts. This idea is based on the principle that our thoughts have a profound impact on our emotions, behaviors, and ultimately, the events and circumstances of our lives.

One way to understand this concept is to think about the idea of attraction. Like attracts like, so if we focus our thoughts on positive, uplifting things, we will attract more positive experiences and outcomes into our lives. On the other hand, if we focus on negative, destructive thoughts, we are likely to attract more negative experiences and outcomes.

It's important to note that this concept does not mean that we can simply wish for things to happen and they will magically appear. Rather, it means that our thoughts shape our beliefs, attitudes, and behaviors, which then influence the actions we take and the results we achieve.

To create the reality we want, it's crucial to focus on positive, empowering thoughts and beliefs, and to take inspired action towards our goals and desires. This requires consistent effort and practice, as our thoughts can often become automatic and negative. However, with time and patience, it is possible to train our minds to focus on what we want and to cultivate a more positive outlook on life.

So, I bet you are asking how the hell am I supposed to focus on positivity, good vibrations, and empowering thoughts when I'm living in a world of shit... (all the stuff you picked this book up for).

The trick is to FOCUS on what you desire so that it GROWS and NOT focus on where you ARE, if it's very negative and does not produce a positive feeling and thinking.

Not to say you should ignore what is going on around you, of course not, take action to get through and feel better, but don't focus on it... FOCUS FORWARD.

The idea that our thoughts create our reality is a powerful one that can have a profound impact on our lives. By focusing on positive, empowering thoughts and taking inspired action, we can shape our experiences and create the reality we want.

CHAPTER THREE

VISUALIZATION

Imagination is everything. It is the preview of life's coming attractions.

– Albert Einstein

Visualization is a mental technique that involves using imagination and positive thoughts to create a vivid picture of a desired outcome or future reality. It is a powerful tool for personal growth and achievement, as it can help you clarify your goals, boost motivation, and increase your chances of success.

Some benefits of visualization include:

- **Increased motivation:** Visualizing your goals can help you tap into your subconscious mind, boost motivation, and increase your drive to achieve your desired outcomes.
- **Improved focus:** By visualizing your goals regularly, you can maintain a clear and focused mind and stay on track towards achieving your desired outcomes.

- **Increased self-belief:** By seeing yourself in your mind's eye as having already achieved your goals, visualization can help you develop a greater sense of self-belief and confidence.
- **Improved performance:** Research has shown that visualization can improve performance in areas such as sports, public speaking, and even academic performance.

To practice visualization, you can follow these steps:

- **Choose a goal:** Decide what you want to achieve and set a clear and specific goal.
- **Create a vivid image:** Close your eyes and create a vivid mental image of yourself achieving your goal. Focus on the details and make the image as vivid and realistic as possible.
- **Focus on positive feelings:** As you visualize your goal, focus on the positive feelings and emotions associated with achieving it.
- **Repeat regularly:** Repeat the visualization process regularly, ideally every day, to reinforce the positive thought patterns and increase the chances of achieving your desired outcomes.
- I find guided visualization videos I've found on YouTube to be an amazing way to complete this with ease!

By incorporating visualization into your daily routine, you can harness its power to bring about positive change and achieve your goals, regardless of the challenges you may face along the way.

SEE IT, BELIEVE IT, ACHIEVE IT!

CHAPTER FOUR

AWARENESS

Look forward to where you want to be and spend no time complaining about where you are.

– Esther Hicks

WATCH OUT FOR THAT NEGATIVE SELF-TALK!

Awareness is one of the MOST IMPORTANT steps in this journey. So many people walk around almost unconscious or like sleepwalking through life. I used to do this too! This book is not about shaming you or putting you down. It's about WAKING YOU UP AND LIFTING YOU UP to the powerful, beautiful human being you are. So many of us are conditioned to just be "average," and if you take a look around, the average person is miserable most of the time, complaining about their life, their mate, their job, kids, the weather, YOU NAME IT!! You don't want to be "average," do you?

Awareness of our thoughts is a crucial aspect of creating the reality we want. It's the first step in taking control of our minds and shaping our beliefs, attitudes, and ultimately, our experiences. When we become aware of our thoughts, we can observe them objectively, without judgment. This allows us to identify negative thought patterns and replace them with positive, empowering ones. It also helps us to recognize when our thoughts are not serving us and to shift our focus towards what we truly want.

Awareness of our thoughts also enables us to cultivate mindfulness and presence in the moment. By focusing on the present moment and becoming aware of our thoughts and emotions, we can reduce stress and increase our overall well-being.

Awareness of our thoughts is a key aspect of creating the reality we want. By becoming mindful and present in the moment, we can observe our thoughts objectively, identify negative patterns, and shift our focus towards what we truly want.

It is extremely important to be aware of how you think and show up in the world to create change and improvement in your life.

CHAPTER FIVE

THE POWER OF I AM…

I am the master of my own destiny, so I choose greatness and nothing less.

– Chiara Gizzi

The words "I am" are incredibly powerful as they shape our beliefs, attitudes, and ultimately, our experiences. These two simple words can influence the way we think about ourselves, the way we interact with the world, and the results we achieve.

When we use the words "I am" to describe ourselves, we are affirming our identity and reinforcing our beliefs. For example, if we say "I am successful," we are affirming that success is a part of our identity and that we believe we can achieve it. On the other hand, if we say "I am a failure," we are reinforcing a negative belief about ourselves and limiting our potential for success.

It's important to be mindful of the words we use when describing ourselves, as they can have a profound impact on our thoughts, emotions, and behavior. By using positive, empowering words, we can cultivate a more positive self-image, increase our self-confidence, and achieve our goals.

The words "I am" are incredibly powerful and have the ability to shape our beliefs, attitudes, and experiences. By using positive, empowering words, we can create a more positive self-image, increase our self-confidence, and achieve our goals.

Some examples of negative thinking I AMs. Let's steer away from negative!

I am stupid
I am fat
I am ugly
I am no good
I am weak
I am nothing without her/him

Some examples of POSITIVE I AMs:

I am ok as I am, and I am improving every day
I am kind
I am deserving of all I desire
I am allowed to be me
I am smart
I am able to figure things out
I am grateful

CHAPTER SIX

STOP GIVING YOUR POWER AWAY

We do not need magic to transform our world. We carry all of the power we need inside ourselves already.

– J. K. Rowling

Giving your power away refers to the act of surrendering control over your life to external factors or people. This can result in feelings of helplessness, low self-esteem, and decreased personal autonomy.

It's important to stop giving your power away because taking control of your life and making your own decisions empowers you to live a more fulfilling and authentic life. By doing so, you can improve your self-esteem, increase your sense of personal autonomy, and cultivate greater happiness and well-being.

What does it mean to give my power away?

Giving someone else the power over your happiness, self-worth, and life… basically relying on another human being to be your end-all, be-all for ALL YOU WANT IN YOUR LIFE! It's a big no-no! We are put on this earth to make ourselves happy. Then connect with others who are happy.

Here are some ways to stop giving your power away:

- **Practice self-awareness:** Take time to reflect on your thoughts and emotions and identify any patterns of surrendering control.
- **Set boundaries:** Learn to say "no" when you need to and establish healthy boundaries to protect your time, energy, and well-being.
- **Take responsibility:** Accept responsibility for your actions and decisions and acknowledge the role you play in your life experiences.
- **Cultivate self-confidence:** Believe in yourself and your abilities and take small steps to build self-confidence.
- **Seek support:** Surround yourself with supportive individuals who encourage and empower you, and seek support when you need it.

CHAPTER SEVEN

ACCOUNTABILITY

*Keep your mind fixed on what you want in life,
not on what you don't want.*

– Napoleon Hill

Accountability for ourselves is an important aspect of creating the reality we want. It involves taking responsibility for our thoughts, beliefs, attitudes, and actions, and committing to making positive changes in our lives.

When we take accountability for ourselves, we empower ourselves to make the necessary changes in our lives to create the reality we want. We acknowledge that we have the power to shape our experiences and that we are responsible for the outcomes we achieve. This mindset can lead to greater self-awareness, personal growth, and a more fulfilling life.

However, taking accountability for ourselves also requires self-discipline and commitment. It's not enough to simply be aware of our thoughts and take responsibility for them. We must also take action to cultivate positive habits and behaviors, and to consistently work towards our goals.

Accountability for ourselves is a critical component of creating the reality we want. By taking responsibility for our thoughts, beliefs, attitudes, and actions, and committing to positive change, we can empower ourselves to shape our experiences and create a more fulfilling life.

The blame game is a common tendency to shift responsibility and avoid accountability for one's own actions and decisions. When someone plays the blame game, they often point the finger at others, deflect criticism, and avoid taking responsibility for their mistakes.

However, playing the blame game has several negative consequences. It undermines personal growth and development, as it prevents individuals from learning from their mistakes and taking responsibility for their actions. It also erodes trust in relationships, as it creates a perception of dishonesty and lack of accountability.

Moreover, playing the blame game can be harmful to one's mental health, as it can increase feelings of guilt, shame, and low self-esteem.

In contrast, taking responsibility and accountability for our actions and decisions is a positive step towards personal growth and development. It demonstrates maturity and integrity, and allows us to learn from our mistakes and make positive changes in our lives.

Therefore, it's important to recognize when we're playing the blame game and to make a conscious effort to take responsibility for our actions and decisions. By doing so, we can cultivate a sense of personal responsibility, improve our relationships, and create a more fulfilling life.

Taking responsibility is actually TAKING YOUR POWER BACK!

CHAPTER EIGHT

ALIGNMENT

See yourself living in abundance, and you will attract it.

– Rhonda Byrne

Alignment with positive or negative refers to the degree to which an individual's thoughts, emotions, and behaviors align with either positive or negative experiences and outcomes.

It also means being aligned with your soul—your true self, your inner being.

When a person is aligned with self and positive experiences, they tend to have a more positive outlook on life and a greater tendency to focus on the good things in their life. This can lead to increased happiness, better relationships, and improved well-being.

In contrast, when a person is NOT aligned with their inner being and only with negative experiences, they tend to focus on the negative aspects of their life and have a more negative outlook. This can lead to feelings of sadness, anxiety, and decreased well-being.

It's important to strive for inner positive alignment, as this can have a positive impact on one's mental and emotional health, relationships, and overall quality of life. However, it's also important to acknowledge and process negative experiences and emotions in a healthy and constructive manner.

By focusing on positive experiences and engaging in practices that promote positive alignment, such as gratitude, mindfulness, and self-care, individuals can improve their overall well-being and lead a more fulfilling life.

CHAPTER NINE

WHO ARE YOU? THE TRUE AUTHENTIC YOU

Decide what you want. Believe you can have it. Believe you deserve it and believe it's possible for you.

– Jack Canfield

Discovering and defining one's own authentic self can be a process of self-exploration and introspection. It involves understanding and accepting one's values, beliefs, and personality, and being true to them in thoughts and actions.

Some ways to begin this process include:

- Reflecting on your values and beliefs
- Engaging in self-reflection and introspection
- Engaging in activities that bring you joy and fulfillment
- Surrounding yourself with supportive individuals who encourage your personal growth

- Practicing self-compassion and self-love

By taking the time to engage in this process of self-discovery, individuals can learn to embrace their authentic selves and lead a more fulfilling and meaningful life.

A good question to ask yourself is:

Is this a conditioned belief or my own belief? Where is this belief coming from?

What do I like to do in my free time? What can I talk about for hours?

What am I passionate about?

Sometimes, we don't even know ourselves, so these self-reflective questions can be hard to answer. Give yourself time, get to know yourself. (And LOVE yourself!)

CHAPTER TEN

ACTION

Whatever the mind can conceive, it can achieve.

– W. Clement Stone

Give up your addiction to excuses and take action!

Taking action for yourself refers to the act of taking steps to improve your life and achieve your goals, rather than waiting for external factors or other people to make things happen for you.

Taking action for yourself is important because it empowers you to shape your own life experiences and bring about positive change. It also helps you develop a sense of agency and personal autonomy, which can improve your self-esteem and overall well-being.

Here are some ways to take action for yourself:

- **Set clear goals:** Identify what you want to achieve and set realistic and attainable goals for yourself.
- **Make a plan:** Break your goals down into smaller, manageable steps and create a plan for achieving them.
- **Take small steps:** Don't be afraid to start small and take consistent, incremental steps towards your goals.
- **Stay focused:** Stay focused on your goals and resist the temptation to give up or become discouraged.
- **Seek support:** Surround yourself with supportive individuals who encourage and empower you, and seek support when you need it.

I teach to take your day 15 minutes at a time if you start to feel overwhelmed.

By taking action for yourself and making progress towards your goals, you can live a more fulfilling and empowered life, and experience the satisfaction and sense of accomplishment that comes from personal growth and achievement.

Failure is only feedback. Success is inevitable, as long as you do not give up. Simple as that.

CHAPTER ELEVEN

GRATITUDE

Be thankful for what you have, you'll end up having more. If you concentrate on what you don't have, you will never ever have enough.

– Oprah Winfrey

Gratitude is an instant feel-good vibrate higher trick. This is one of THE MOST IMPORTANT STEPS to do daily!

I've saved the best for last!

Gratitude is the act of being thankful and appreciative for the good things in life. Research has shown that practicing gratitude can have significant benefits for mental and emotional well-being, relationships, and overall life satisfaction.

Some benefits of gratitude include:

- **Increased happiness:** Gratitude helps shift focus from negative experiences to positive ones, leading to increased feelings of happiness and well-being.

- **Improved relationships:** Expressing gratitude can strengthen relationships, improve communication, and increase feelings of connectedness.
- **Decreased stress and anxiety:** Gratitude has been shown to decrease stress and anxiety, as it helps individuals focus on the good things in their lives rather than dwelling on the negative.
- **Enhanced resilience:** Gratitude can help individuals develop a more positive outlook on life and become more resilient in the face of adversity.
- **Better sleep:** Gratitude has been shown to improve sleep quality, as it promotes a sense of peace and contentment.

There are several ways to practice gratitude, such as:

- **Keeping a gratitude journal:** Write down things that you're grateful for each day. I suggest starting with 3 or 4 things that you are grateful for, preferably in the morning.
- **Expressing gratitude to others:** Write thank you notes, give compliments, or express appreciation to those around you.
- **Practicing mindfulness:** Take time to focus on the present moment and appreciate the good things in your life.
- **Engaging in acts of kindness:** Doing something kind for others can help increase feelings of gratitude.

I also suggest holding onto that "feel-good gratitude" feeling that you receive while writing in your journal (or even thinking of the few things you are grateful for) throughout the day, especially when you start to feel yourself drift towards negative thinking, revert back to that gratitude feeling.

By incorporating gratitude into daily life, individuals can reap its many benefits and lead a more fulfilling and joyful life. It is IMPOSSIBLE to feel sadness, frustration, anxiety, stress, etc., all the negative feelings and emotions when you are feeling gratitude. Hence, it is one of the most important things to implement into your life DAILY to feel good and happy immediately!

CONCLUSION

As you can see from what I explained in this book, YOUR HAPPINESS STARTS WITH YOU!

YOU are the only one who has the power to create it!

Within you IS the MAGIC PLACE!

Once you take your power back and truly learn to love and respect YOURSELF, you will attract and obtain all you desire!

With the steps learned in this book, you now have a baseline to go forward in your life with the knowledge and awareness of where to start.

Attaining your goals and desires will definitely be fast-tracked if you work with a mentor or life coach who has gone through similar life experiences to what you are going through AND who has the success and dream life you seek!

It's very important to have someone who can truly support you with what you have learned, hold you accountable, and assure you along your journey.

With these core concepts, YOU CANNOT FAIL!

Interested in learning more about me and/or working with me to help you implement this guide into your life?

Come into my world!!! Here are my links:

Email: Elisemorgan@coachelisemorgan.com

Instagram: @elisemorganexperience

Podcast: "The Elise Morgan Experience"

Bonus Journal

Unveiling the inner power of YOU!

Dear Reader,

Congratulations on completing THE MAGIC PLACE. To extend the adventure, I've included a bonus journal for you.

Within these pages, you'll find space for your reflections. This journal is an invitation to delve into your thoughts, dreams, and experiences. Whether you're a seasoned journal writer or just starting out, let it be a canvas for your unique journey.

I've also added some prompts to help you along.

May this journal amplify the power of you, your story, and your life.

Happy journaling!

***** If you have the ebook version of THE MAGIC PLACE, please use the following journal pages as a guide and template to use in a notebook or journal of your choice, since you are unable to write in the journal provided.

Here are some I AM journal prompts to use, or you can create your own.

In the beginning, it may feel awkward to do this practice or to feel what you are writing.

Pick the ones that feel the most true for you.

I am worthy of love and respect.

I am capable of achieving my goals.

I am grateful for the abundance in my life.

I am confident and believe in my abilities.

I am constantly evolving and growing.

I am surrounded by positivity and good energy.

I am in control of my thoughts and emotions.

I am deserving of success and happiness.

I am a magnet for miracles and opportunities.

I am proud of the progress I've made.

I am a source of inspiration for others.

I am aligned with my purpose and passions.

I am open to new possibilities and adventures.

I am attracting positive relationships into my life.

I am at peace with my past and excited for my future.

I am resilient and can overcome any challenges.

I am a beacon of light and positivity.

I am mindful and present in each moment.

I am deserving of self-care and relaxation.

I am a valuable and irreplaceable individual.

I am choosing happiness and joy every day.

Here are some one-word affirmations that you can use after the words I AM:

Worthy	Capable
Grateful	Confident
Evolving	Positive
Control	Deserving
Miracles	Proud
Inspire	Aligned
Open	Great Relationships
Peace	Resilient
Light	Mindful
Self-Care	Valuable
Joyful	

FOR THE "I AM GRATEFUL" AFFIRMATIONS:

As suggested in the GRATITUDE chapter, I suggest picking 3–4 things you are grateful for.

WRITE THEM DOWN. FEEL THEM.

REALLY FEEL THE GRATITUDE!

For when you are feeling grateful, it is impossible to feel angry, sad, lost, anxious, ALL the negative vibration feelings.

GRATITUDE is a very HIGH vibrational feeling.

Try this affirmation/gratitude journaling with the FREE journal included for AT LEAST 21 DAYS. It takes approximately 21 days to form a habit and improve thought.

In addition to the journaling, SAY these affirmations to yourself throughout the day to keep your vibration and "frequency" high.

Remember, like attracts like…

What you think and feel, you ATTRACT!

Gratitude Journal

Date: ../../....

Today, I'm grateful for:
- ....
- ....
- ....

I am inspired to take action on this:

....
....
....

Today's affirmation and I ams:
- ....
- ....
- ....
- ....

Notes & Reminders:

THE MAGIC PLACE

Gratitude Journal

Date: ../../....

Today, I'm grateful for:
- ....
- ....
- ....

I am inspired to take action on this:
....
....
....

Today's affirmation and I ams:
- ....
- ....
- ....
- ....

Notes & Reminders:

Gratitude Journal

Date: ../../....

Today, I'm grateful for:
- ....
- ....
- ....

I am inspired to take action on this:

....
....
....

Today's affirmation and I ams:
- ....
- ....
- ....
- ....

Notes & Reminders:

THE MAGIC PLACE

Gratitude Journal

Date: ../../....

Today, I'm grateful for:
- ....
- ....
- ....

I am inspired to take action on this:

....
....
....

Today's affirmation and I ams:
- ....
- ....
- ....
- ....

Notes & Reminders:

Gratitude Journal

Date: ../../....

Today, I'm grateful for:
- ....
- ....
- ....

I am inspired to take action on this:

....
....
....

Today's affirmation and I ams:
- ....
- ....
- ....
- ....

Notes & Reminders:

Gratitude Journal

Date: ../../....

Today, I'm grateful for:
- ....
- ....
- ....

I am inspired to take action on this:
....
....
....

Today's affirmation and I ams:
- ....
- ....
- ....
- ....

Notes & Reminders:

Gratitude Journal

Date: ../../....

Today, I'm grateful for:
- ....
- ....
- ....

I am inspired to take action on this:

....
....
....

Today's affirmation and I ams:
- ....
- ....
- ....
- ....

Notes & Reminders:

Gratitude Journal

Date: ../../....

Today, I'm grateful for:
- ....
- ....
- ....

I am inspired to take action on this:

....
....
....

Today's affirmation and I ams:
- ....
- ....
- ....
- ....

Notes & Reminders:

Gratitude Journal

Date: ../../....

Today, I'm grateful for:
- ....
- ....
- ....

I am inspired to take action on this:

....

....

....

Today's affirmation and I ams:
- ....
- ....
- ....
- ....

Notes & Reminders:

Gratitude Journal

Date: ../../....

Today, I'm grateful for:
- ....
- ....
- ....

I am inspired to take action on this:
....
....
....

Today's affirmation and I ams:
- ....
- ....
- ....
- ....

Notes & Reminders:

Gratitude Journal

Date: ../../....

Today, I'm grateful for:
- ....
- ....
- ....

I am inspired to take action on this:
....
....
....

Today's affirmation and I ams:
- ....
- ....
- ....
- ....

Notes & Reminders:

THE MAGIC PLACE

Gratitude Journal

Date: ../../....

Today, I'm grateful for:
- ....
- ....
- ....

I am inspired to take action on this:
....
....
....

Today's affirmation and I ams:
- ....
- ....
- ....
- ....

Notes & Reminders:

Gratitude Journal

Date: ../../....

Today, I'm grateful for:
- ....
- ....
- ....

I am inspired to take action on this:

....
....
....

Today's affirmation and I ams:
- ....
- ....
- ....
- ....

Notes & Reminders:

Gratitude Journal

Date: ../../....

Today, I'm grateful for:
- ....
- ....
- ....

I am inspired to take action on this:

....
....
....

Today's affirmation and I ams:
- ....
- ....
- ....
- ....

Notes & Reminders:

Gratitude Journal

Date: ../../....

Today, I'm grateful for:
- ....
- ....
- ....

I am inspired to take action on this:

....
....
....

Today's affirmation and I ams:
- ....
- ....
- ....
- ....

Notes & Reminders:

THE MAGIC PLACE

Gratitude Journal

Date: ../../....

Today, I'm grateful for:
- ....
- ....
- ....

I am inspired to take action on this:

....
....
....

Today's affirmation and I ams:
- ....
- ....
- ....
- ....

Notes & Reminders:

Gratitude Journal

Date: ../../....

Today, I'm grateful for:
- ....
- ....
- ....

I am inspired to take action on this:

....
....
....

Today's affirmation and I ams:
- ....
- ....
- ....
- ....

Notes & Reminders:

Gratitude Journal

Date: ../../....

Today, I'm grateful for:
- ....
- ....
- ....

I am inspired to take action on this:

....
....
....

Today's affirmation and I ams:
- ....
- ....
- ....
- ....

Notes & Reminders:

Gratitude Journal

Date: ../../....

Today, I'm grateful for:
- ....
- ....
- ....

I am inspired to take action on this:

....
....
....

Today's affirmation and I ams:
- ....
- ....
- ....
- ....

Notes & Reminders:

THE MAGIC PLACE

Gratitude Journal

Date: ../../....

Today, I'm grateful for:
- ....
- ....
- ....

I am inspired to take action on this:

....
....
....

Today's affirmation and I ams:
- ....
- ....
- ....
- ....

Notes & Reminders:

Gratitude Journal

Date: ../../....

Today, I'm grateful for:
- ....
- ....
- ....

I am inspired to take action on this:

....
....
....

Today's affirmation and I ams:
- ....
- ....
- ....
- ....

Notes & Reminders:

Gratitude Journal

Date: ../../....

Today, I'm grateful for:
- ....
- ....
- ....

I am inspired to take action on this:

....
....
....

Today's affirmation and I ams:
- ....
- ....
- ....
- ....

Notes & Reminders:

Gratitude Journal

Date: ../../....

Today, I'm grateful for:
- ....
- ....
- ....

I am inspired to take action on this:

....
....
....

Today's affirmation and I ams:
- ....
- ....
- ....
- ....

Notes & Reminders:

Gratitude Journal

Date: ../../....

Today, I'm grateful for:
- ....
- ....
- ....

I am inspired to take action on this:

....
....
....

Today's affirmation and I ams:
- ....
- ....
- ....
- ....

Notes & Reminders:

Gratitude Journal

Date: ../../....

Today, I'm grateful for:
- ....
- ....
- ....

I am inspired to take action on this:

....
....
....

Today's affirmation and I ams:
- ....
- ....
- ....
- ....

Notes & Reminders:

Gratitude Journal

Date: ../../....

Today, I'm grateful for:
- ....
- ....
- ....

I am inspired to take action on this:
....
....
....

Today's affirmation and I ams:
- ....
- ....
- ....
- ....

Notes & Reminders:

Gratitude Journal

Date: ../../....

Today, I'm grateful for:
- ....
- ....
- ....

I am inspired to take action on this:

....
....
....

Today's affirmation and I ams:
- ....
- ....
- ....
- ....

Notes & Reminders:

THE MAGIC PLACE

Gratitude Journal

Date: ../../....

Today, I'm grateful for:
- ....
- ....
- ....

I am inspired to take action on this:

....
....
....

Today's affirmation and I ams:
- ....
- ....
- ....
- ....

Notes & Reminders:

Gratitude Journal

Date: ../../....

Today, I'm grateful for:
- ....
- ....
- ....

I am inspired to take action on this:

....
....
....

Today's affirmation and I ams:
- ....
- ....
- ....
- ....

Notes & Reminders:

THE MAGIC PLACE

Gratitude Journal

Date: ../../....

Today, I'm grateful for:
- ....
- ....
- ....

I am inspired to take action on this:

....
....
....

Today's affirmation and I ams:
- ....
- ....
- ....
- ....

Notes & Reminders:

Gratitude Journal

Date: ../../....

Today, I'm grateful for:
- ....
- ....
- ....

I am inspired to take action on this:

....
....
....

Today's affirmation and I ams:
- ....
- ....
- ....
- ....

Notes & Reminders:

Gratitude Journal

Date: ../../....

Today, I'm grateful for:
- ....
- ....
- ....

I am inspired to take action on this:
....
....
....

Today's affirmation and I ams:
- ....
- ....
- ....
- ....

Notes & Reminders:

Gratitude Journal

Date: ../../....

Today, I'm grateful for:
- ....
- ....
- ....

I am inspired to take action on this:
....
....
....

Today's affirmation and I ams:
- ....
- ....
- ....
- ....

Notes & Reminders:

THE MAGIC PLACE

Gratitude Journal

Date: ../../....

Today, I'm grateful for:
- ....
- ....
- ....

I am inspired to take action on this:

....
....
....

Today's affirmation and I ams:
- ....
- ....
- ....
- ....

Notes & Reminders:

Gratitude Journal

Date: ../../....

Today, I'm grateful for:
- ....
- ....
- ....

I am inspired to take action on this:

....
....
....

Today's affirmation and I ams:
- ....
- ....
- ....
- ....

Notes & Reminders:

Gratitude Journal

Date: ../../....

Today, I'm grateful for:
- ....
- ....
- ....

I am inspired to take action on this:

....
....
....

Today's affirmation and I ams:
- ....
- ....
- ....
- ....

Notes & Reminders:

Gratitude Journal

Date: ../../....

Today, I'm grateful for:
- ....
- ....
- ....

I am inspired to take action on this:

....
....
....

Today's affirmation and I ams:
- ....
- ....
- ....
- ....

Notes & Reminders:

THE MAGIC PLACE

Gratitude Journal

Date: ../../....

Today, I'm grateful for:
- ....
- ....
- ....

I am inspired to take action on this:

....
....
....

Today's affirmation and I ams:
- ....
- ....
- ....
- ....

Notes & Reminders:

Gratitude Journal

Date: ../../....

Today, I'm grateful for:
- ....
- ....
- ....

I am inspired to take action on this:

....
....
....

Today's affirmation and I ams:
- ....
- ....
- ....
- ....

Notes & Reminders:

Gratitude Journal

Date: ../../....

Today, I'm grateful for:
- ....
- ....
- ....

I am inspired to take action on this:

....
....
....

Today's affirmation and I ams:
- ....
- ....
- ....
- ....

Notes & Reminders:

Gratitude Journal

Date: ../../....

Today, I'm grateful for:
- ....
- ....
- ....

I am inspired to take action on this:
....
....
....

Today's affirmation and I ams:
- ....
- ....
- ....
- ....

Notes & Reminders:

Gratitude Journal

Date: ../../....

Today, I'm grateful for:
- ....
- ....
- ....

I am inspired to take action on this:

....
....
....

Today's affirmation and I ams:
- ....
- ....
- ....
- ....

Notes & Reminders:

Gratitude Journal

Date: ../../....

Today, I'm grateful for:
- ....
- ....
- ....

I am inspired to take action on this:

....
....
....

Today's affirmation and I ams:
- ....
- ....
- ....
- ....

Notes & Reminders:

Gratitude Journal

Date: ../../....

Today, I'm grateful for:
- ....
- ....
- ....

I am inspired to take action on this:

....
....
....

Today's affirmation and I ams:
- ....
- ....
- ....
- ....

Notes & Reminders:

Gratitude Journal

Date: ../../....

Today, I'm grateful for:
- ....
- ....
- ....

I am inspired to take action on this:

....
....
....

Today's affirmation and I ams:
- ....
- ....
- ....
- ....

Notes & Reminders:

THE MAGIC PLACE

Gratitude Journal

Date: ../../....

Today, I'm grateful for:
- ....
- ....
- ....

I am inspired to take action on this:
....
....
....

Today's affirmation and I ams:
- ....
- ....
- ....
- ....

Notes & Reminders:

Gratitude Journal

Date: ../../....

Today, I'm grateful for:
- ....
- ....
- ....

I am inspired to take action on this:

....
....
....

Today's affirmation and I ams:
- ....
- ....
- ....
- ....

Notes & Reminders:

THE MAGIC PLACE

Gratitude Journal

Date: ../../....

Today, I'm grateful for:
- ....
- ....
- ....

I am inspired to take action on this:

....
....
....

Today's affirmation and I ams:
- ....
- ....
- ....
- ....

Notes & Reminders:

www.ingramcontent.com/pod-product-compliance
Lightning Source LLC
Chambersburg PA
CBHW042054060526
44107CB00154B/1027